Olympic Greats

# OLYMPIC VOLLEYBALL LEGENDS

MARTIN GITLIN

BLACK RABBIT BOOKS

Bolt is published by Black Rabbit Books
P.O. Box 3263, Mankato, Minnesota, 56002.
www.blackrabbitbooks.com


Jen Besel, editor; Catherine Cates, designer;
Omay Ayres, photo researcher



Library of Congress Cataloging-in-Publication Data
Names: Gitlin, Marty, author.
Title: Olympic volleyball legends / by Martin Gitlin.
Other titles: Bolt (North Mankato, Minn.)
Description: Mankato, Minnesota : Bolt is published by Black Rabbit Books, 2021.| Series: Bolt. Olympic greats | Includes webography. | Includes bibliographic references and index. | Audience: Ages: 8-12 years. |Audience: Grades: 4-6.
Identifiers: LCCN 2019028642 (print) | ISBN 9781623102692 (Hardcover) | ISBN 9781644663653 (Paperback) | ISBN 9781623103637 (eBook)
Subjects: LCSH: Volleyball players—Juvenile literature. | Volleyball—Records. | Olympics—Juvenile literature.
Classification: LCC GV1015.34 .G58 2021 (print) | LCC GV1015.34 (ebook) | DDC 796.325—dc23
LC record available at https://lccn.loc.gov/2019028642
LC ebook record available at https://lccn.loc.gov/2019028643

Printed in the United States. 2/20

**All statistics are through the 2016 Olympic Games.**

**Image Credits**
Alamy: Filippo Rubin, 1; Jack Sullivan, 13, 17, 21, 24, 28–29 (medal); ZUMA Press, 25 (b); AP Images: BETH A. KEISER, 11; BOB GALBRAITH, 15 (main); Dave Martin, 25 (t); JONNE RORIZ, 12; Koji Sasahara, 26; Margaret Bowles, 16–17 (main); enews.tech: enews, 7; fivb.org: FIVB, 22; Newscom: Nhat V. Meyer, 4–5;Sho Tamura, Cover; YVES HERMAN, 14 (main); Shutterstock: Alex Emanuel Koch, 3 (net); Anton Shaparenko, 8–9 (icons); Anucha Tiemsom, 8 (court); Aptyp_koK, 3, 32 (ball); kapona, 31; kstudija, 18–19 (figures); Nata-Art, 6, 10, 15, 20 (medals); Paul Crash, 8–9, 14, 23, 27, 29 (rings); Ron Dale, 9 (sand); womenofchina.cn: Joyce Dong, 21 (main)
Every effort has been made to contact copyright holders for material reproduced in this book. Any omissions will be rectified in subsequent printings if notice is given to the publisher.

# CONTENTS

MIKASA

# Amazing ATHLETES

They jump high. They slam the ball. They dive to the ground. Volleyball players are amazing athletes. The world's best compete in the Summer Olympics.

The Summer Games are held every four years. Countries send their best players to compete. They **dig** some great action.

# Powerful PLAYERS

## Dusty Dvorak

Dusty Dvorak competed in just one Olympics. But he proved he was one of the greatest **setters** ever. He set the ball where teammates could slam it. Those slams became points. He helped his team win gold.

1
USA

## VOLLEYBALL EVENTS

**The Olympics has two kinds of volleyball. Volleyball is held on an indoor court. Beach volleyball is played outside on sand.**

# BEACH VOLLEYBALL

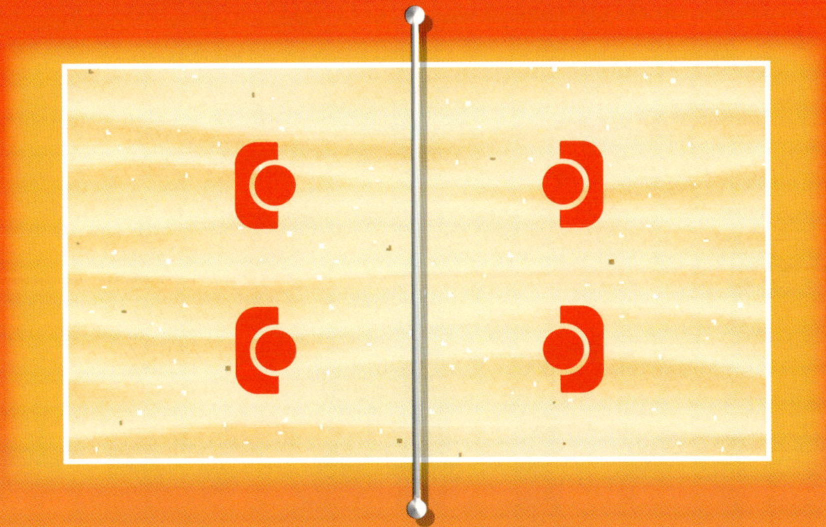

## 2-PLAYER TEAMS

## Ana Ibis Fernandez

Cuba **dominated** women's volleyball for years. Ana Ibis Fernandez was a big reason it did. She won points with her powerful **spikes.** In 2000, she scored at least 10 points in six **matches**.

**Points Scored by Fernandez in 2000 Olympics**

| SEPTEMBER 16 | SEPTEMBER 18 | SEPTEMBER 20 |
|---|---|---|
| 8 points | 5 points | 14 points |

| (finals) | | | | |
|---|---|---|---|---|
| SEPTEMBER 22 | SEPTEMBER 24 | SEPTEMBER 26 | SEPTEMBER 28 | SEPTEMBER 30 (finals) |
| **12** points | **15** points | **10** points | **10** points | **10** points |

His nickname was Giba.

## Gilberto Godoy Filho

Gilberto Godoy Filho was not as tall as many players. But he could spike with force. He scored at least 10 points in 11 straight Olympic matches. He even had an amazing 26-point match in 2004.

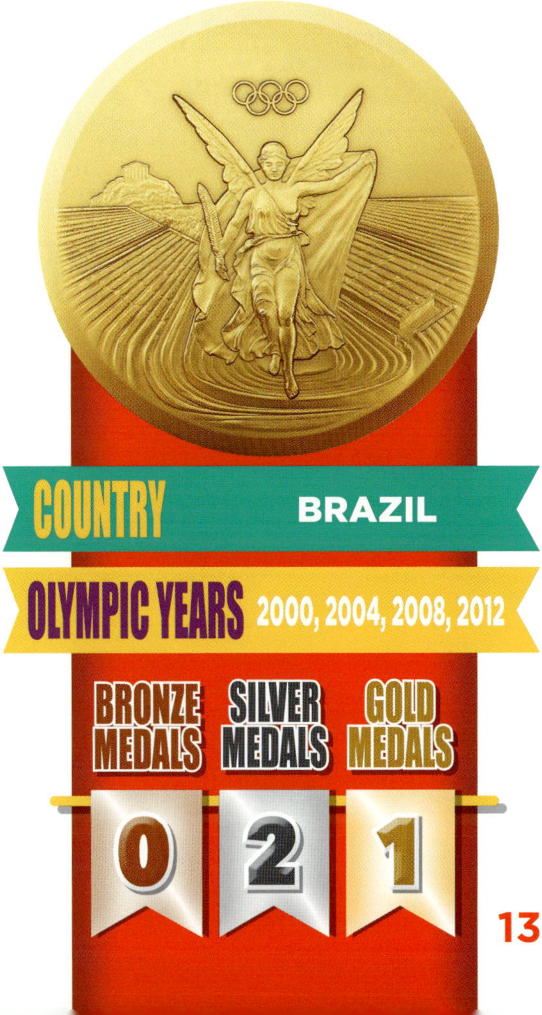

# Osmany Juantorena

Osmany Juantorena is a tall spiker. He slams the ball with force. In the 2016 Games, he scored 90 points from spikes. Nearly half of his total spikes ended in points.

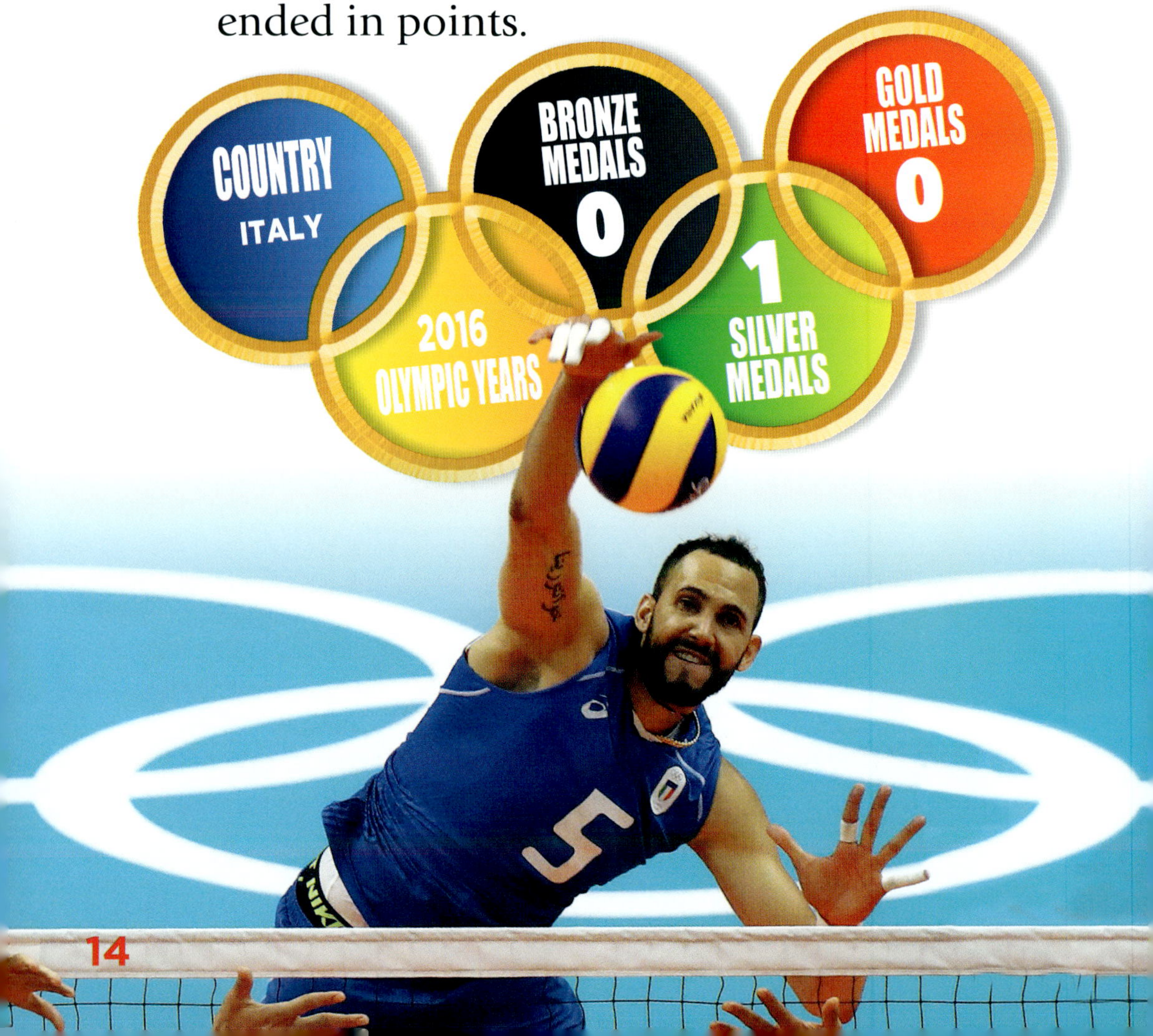

## Karch Kiraly

Karch Kiraly won two gold medals for indoor volleyball. He won another in beach volleyball. Some people think he is the greatest player ever. He could make tough shots. And he **inspired** teammates to play their best.

**COUNTRY** UNITED STATES

**OLYMPIC YEARS** 1984, 1988, 1996

BRONZE MEDALS 0

SILVER MEDALS 0

GOLD MEDALS 3

May-Treanor won the Olympic Most Outstanding Player award in 2004 and 2008.

## Misty May-Treanor

Misty May-Treanor was a powerful beach volleyball player. She didn't make it easy for others to score. May-Treanor teamed up with Kerri Walsh Jennings. They won 21 straight Olympic matches.

# Positions on an Olympic VOLLEYBALL TEAM

**OUTSIDE HITTER**

hits ball from the setter

**MIDDLE BLOCKER**

blocks attacks from the other team

**RIGHT SIDE HITTER**

hits ball from the setter

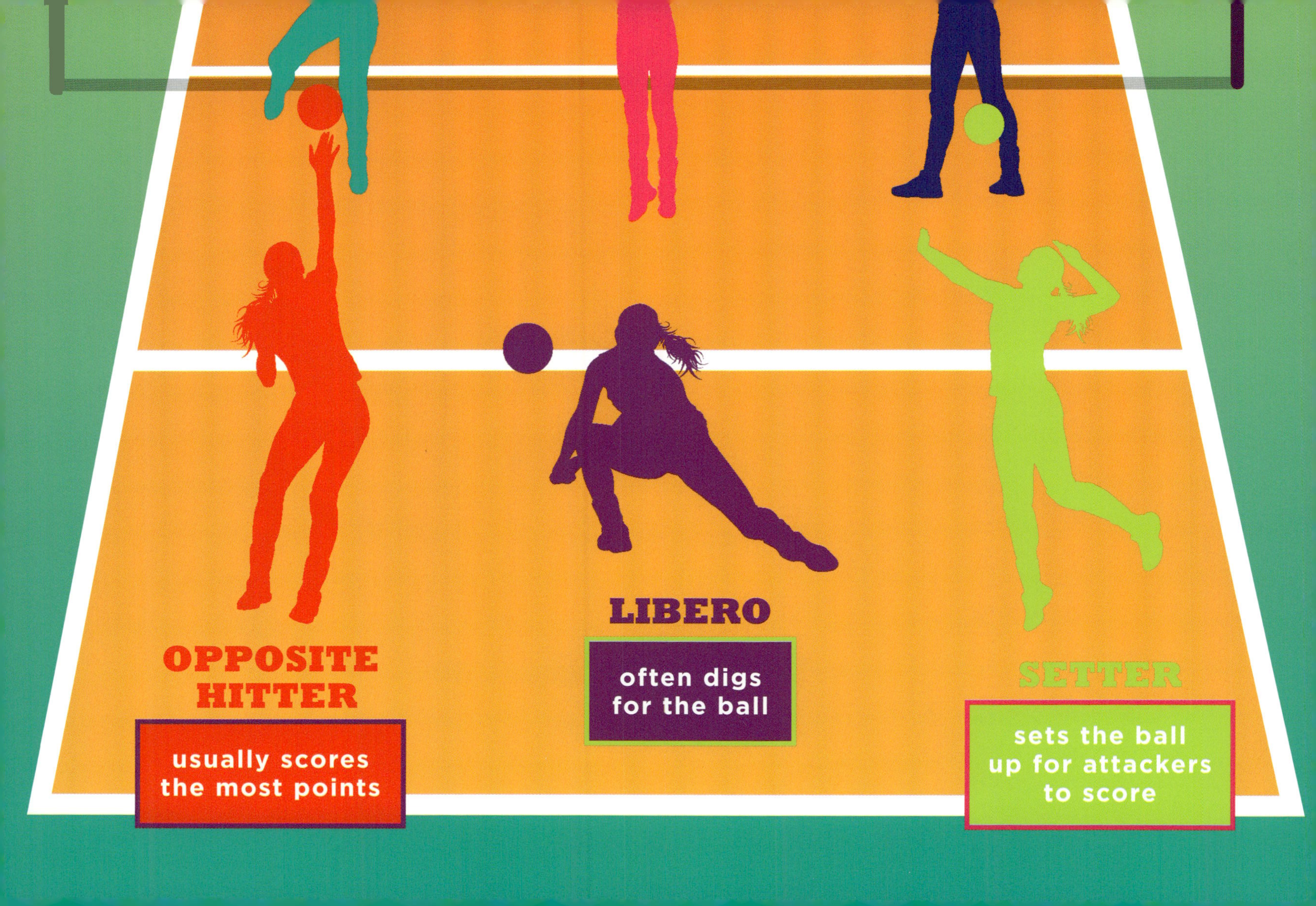
OPPOSITE HITTER
usually scores the most points
LIBERO
often digs for the ball
SETTER
sets the ball up for attackers to score

## Lang Ping

China had strong women's volleyball teams in the 1980s. Lang Ping was one reason why. She was the best outside hitter on the team. She racked up points. Her points helped her team win gold.

## COUNTRIES WITH THE MOST WOMEN'S VOLLEYBALL AND BEACH VOLLEYBALL MEDALS

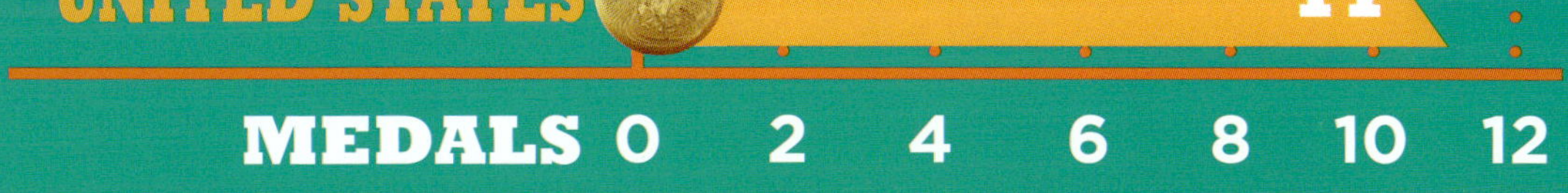

Torres became the youngest volleyball gold medalist in 1992. She was 17 years old.

## Regla Torres

Regla Torres was a great middle blocker and hitter. She was named the Best Female Volleyball Player of the 20th **Century**. She showed her strength in her last Olympic match. Torres scored an incredible 23 points in the 2000 finals.

## Kerri Walsh Jennings

Passion and hard work made Kerri Walsh Jennings a great player. She has played in five Olympics. And she has more medals than any other beach volleyball player.

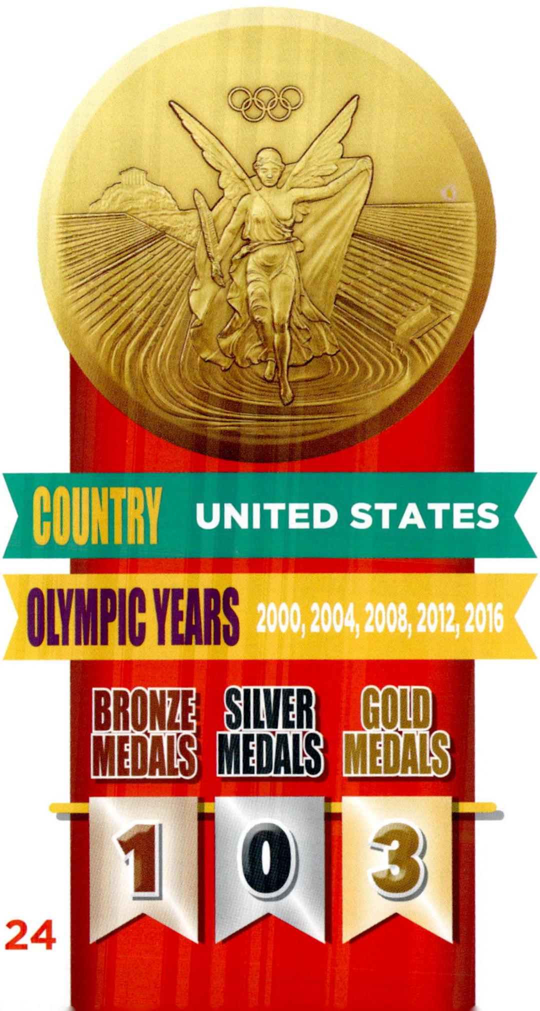

Walsh Jennings and Misty May-Treanor won every Olympic match they played together.

MIKASA

## Kim Yeon-Koung

Kim Yeon-Koung never won an Olympic medal. Her teams weren't strong enough. But her skills made her an Olympic **legend**. She had great force and quick movements. She scored an incredible 185 spike points in the 2012 Olympics.

CHAPTER 3

# Comparing CAREERS

Athletes push to be the best during the Summer Olympics. Compare the stats of some of volleyball's greatest.

## TOTAL MEDALS

# OLYMPIC APPEARANCES

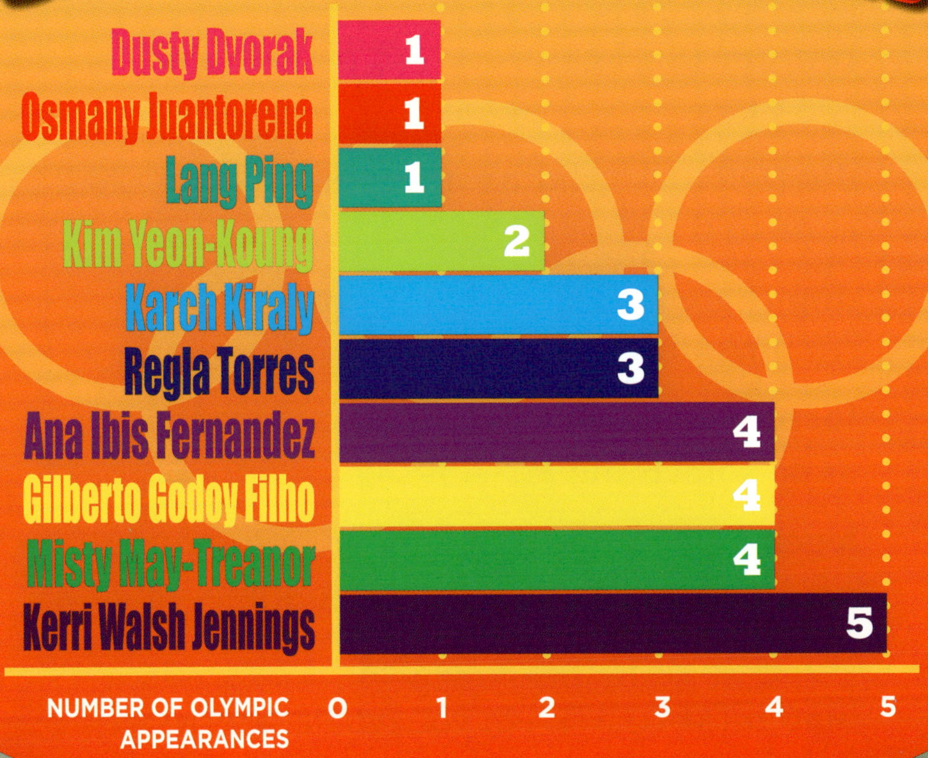

# GLOSSARY

**century** (SEN-chuh-ree)—a period of 100 years

**dig** (DIHG)— sliding under and hitting a ball close to the floor

**dominate** (DOM-uh-neyt)—to hold a commanding position over

**inspire** (in-SPIHR)—to make someone want to do something

**legend** (LEJ-uhnd)—a famous or important person who is known for doing something extremely well

**match** (MATCH)—in volleyball, a series of games played to determine a winner; Olympic matches consist of five games.

**setter** (SET-uhr)—a passer in volleyball whose job is to position a pass to the hitter

**spike** (SPIHK)—a type of attack in volleyball where the ball is hit down over the net with good force and speed

# LEARN MORE

## BOOKS

**Doeden, Matt.** *Volleyball.* Summer Olympic Sports. Mankato, MN: Amicus High Interest, 2016.

**Fretland VanVoorst, Jenny.** *The Science Behind Volleyball.* STEM in the Summer Olympics. Minneapolis: Jump!, Inc., 2020.

**Kortemeier, Todd.** *12 Reasons to Love Volleyball.* Sports Report. Mankato, MN: 12-Story Library, 2018.

## WEBSITES

Beach Volleyball – Summer Olympic Sport
**www.olympic.org/beach-volleyball**

Volleyball – Summer Olympic Sport
**www.olympic.org/volleyball**

What Is Olympic Volleyball?
**www.youtube.com/watch?v=hX6pMHJK3ZM**

# INDEX